SO-AES-321

Wild and Woolly:

A Journal Keeper's

Handbook

Wild and Woolly:
A Journal Keeper's
Handbook

Alfred DePew

Dog Star Press

Portland, Maine USA

www.alfreddepew.com

© 2004

All rights reserved

ISBN 1-929565-09-7

Illustrations by Melissa Sweet

Book and jacket design by Abby Johnston
    and Tim McCreight

All rights reserved. No part of this publication may be
reproduced or transmitted in any form or by any means,
electronic, or mechanical, including photocopying,
recording, or any storage and retrieval system now known
or to be invented, except by a reviewer who wishes to
quote brief passages in connection with a review written for
inclusion in a magazine, newspaper, or broadcast.

Dedication

For Connie Hayes, who, when I proposed
a journal workshop one summer at the
Portland School of Art, said, "Sure.
What the hell?
Let's try it."

And for everyone who keeps
showing up to collaborate.

Table of Contents

People need wild places. Whether or not we think we do, we do. We need to be able to taste grace and know once again that we desire it. We need to experience a landscape that is timeless, whose agenda moves at the pace of speciation and glaciers. To be surrounded by a singing, mating, howling commotion of other species, all of which love their lives as much as we do ours...

— Barbara Kingslover

A Word About Wildness

A number of years ago, I taught a course called the Frontier in American History. We began with the Puritans and read right the way through to Marge Piercey's *Woman on the Edge of Time*, which I saw as a sort of frontier novel. Throughout the semester, we were curious to discover what the frontier had meant to us in our history, both as a metaphor and as political reality. We noticed the Puritan stance toward the wilderness, and how the policy shifted during King Philip's war from trying to make Christians of the indigenous peoples to out-and-out genocide. The Native Americans became evil incarnate in the minds of theologians. Not only must they be destroyed, but where they lived—the forests—must be destroyed (cleared, owned, farmed, fenced, settled) as well.

I've always seen that as a turning point in our history, and if I remember correctly, you can see it in entries in Cotton Mather's journal—almost to the day. It seems to me that this shift in policy has affected us right down to the present, and still, in some ways, guides our land use policy. An oversimplification, perhaps, but there's truth in it nonetheless, I think.

Whatever the reason, or historical roots, today we find ourselves living with a mess. At a time when the very last wilderness areas on earth are threatened by corporate greed, it is more and more important to cultivate our inner wildness. By husbanding one, we husband the other. And until we come to terms with, appreciate, and really come to love the wildness of our own psyches, we will forever be at odds with the wildness of the natural world. So there is a certain urgency about doing our inner work at present.

Some people know what they do, and they do it.
I do what I do , and then I know it.

— Isamu Noguchi

Foreword

I get stuck. Chances are you do too, or you'd be in another part of the bookstore, browsing Auto Mechanics, or Cook Books, or Fiction. But you're here, leafing through this book, thinking you really ought to keep a journal; you've always meant to. Your therapist says it will help you get in touch with your feelings, but you probably wouldn't do it every day, so why bother?

Or you go ahead and buy a blank book—bottom shelf to your left—get it home, open it, pick up a pen, and every thought flies out of your head except one: you have nothing to say. Or you remember eighth grade English class and Mr. Achputch's vocabulary quizzes, ("'I have reached the *acme* of my career!' he *ejaculated* with glee.") compositions returned, covered in red ink: fragment, dangling modifier, pronoun reference, logic, "What exactly is your point here?" Everything wrong. Or maybe you already have half a dozen journals you've begun and abandoned because you never finish anything. Or you think: what if someone finds my diaries when I'm dead, or worse—when I'm still alive!

So you say, "Forget it; it's a stupid idea. Who the hell wants to get in touch with their feelings, anyway? A waste of time." And that's the end of it. At least it has been. Until now.

I invite you to take the plunge, in spite of all your excellent reasons not to. Just pick up your pen or pencil and begin. I'll be right here with you: encouraging, prodding, questioning, provoking, and irritating at every step of the way. Where to begin? How? It doesn't matter. My intent for this handbook is to guide you through exercises I've developed in my journal workshops over the past 13 years. To loosen up and play around. To let go of fear, or wrestle with it; in any case to change your relationship to fear, so you can deepen into more powerful parts of the Self.

Like my workshops, this book is meant for the absolute beginner as well as the seasoned diarist: for artists, coaches, engineers, athletes, gardeners, lawyers, roofers, hairstylists, therapists, students, teachers, masseurs, gurus, dancers, factory workers, movie stars, bosses, dreamers, and practical folk alike. In other words, everybody. And yes, that includes you.

So lighten up. Be willing to be surprised. See how these exercises work for you. If you get bogged down in one chapter, skip to another. Then go back to it later, if you've a mind to. If not, then don't. As they say in the South, "Take what you can use, and let the rest rot." No blame. My intent is for you to be working in your journal in whatever ways are useful to you. I'm passing along exercises that people in my workshops tell me are useful to them, exercises that have been useful to me in my own journal practice—that's all. Try them. See for yourself. And have some fun.

At the same time, you want to establish and maintain a regular practice of keeping a journal. This takes a certain amount of discipline. I'm not talking about nuns with rulers. This has nothing to do with abuse, and yet somehow the two have become linked in our minds, so I'd like to take a moment to separate them again. Our word discipline comes from the Latin *disciplinia, meaning* teaching, learning, and from *discipluus, meaning* pupil. Discipline involves putting time and attention into something we value in order to learn, teach, improve and progress.

Will is involved here.

So is frustration.

So is patience.

Also discovery, satisfaction—even joy.

I'm not sure where we got the notion that everything is supposed to be easy and instant. Whether it's TV or computers or sugar, or all of these, I've noticed in my students at the art school over the past 20 years, a lower tolerance for frustration. I've become convinced that nothing, and certainly not art, gets created without going through periods of frustration. Years ago, one of my drawing teachers at Webster College used to say that those moments of greatest frustration signaled breakthroughs in learning and seeing; that it was important to stay with them and not abandon the drawing, but to keep pushing through.

I'd add to this the importance of making a mess, which so often involves failure and disappointment and maybe even starting over. As a friend used to say, "Anything worth doing is worth doing poorly." I'd add that in order to do anything well, we have to be willing to do it poorly. This is what I tell my writing students and coaching clients again and again.

The difference in journal keeping is that there is no end product. A journal, at least the way I use one, is a process. I am not making art or literature or even anything that I expect to be coherent. However within this process, I discover a great deal about my life and what I feel and how I think. From time to time, I realize things. I follow inklings. I come away learning something new.

So, yes, a journal practice requires a certain amount of discipline. Get curious. Be willing to be surprised. Train yourself to come regularly to this practice, or, as Linda Metcalf used to say, "Make an appointment with yourself. And keep it."

The challenge is to develop the discipline needed, without turning the whole enterprise into a lifeless chore. You want to establish enough forward motion so the practice can sustain itself. That is to say, you need to derive a certain amount of benefit from keeping a journal in order to continue. Once you've seen how useful it can be to spend time with yourself in your notebook, you'll have the incentive to keep going. That's all these exercises are for: to be of use, to help you get started or unstuck, or to help you see a problem or challenge from a new perspective, to help recharge your creativity, and to enable you to go deeper into your own life—now.

Security is mostly a superstition. It does not exist in nature, nor do the children of men as a whole experience it. Avoiding danger is no safer in the long run than outright exposure. Life is either a daring adventure or nothing. To keep our faces toward change and behave like free spirits in the presence of fate is strength undefeatable.

— Helen Keller

Considering how dangerous everything is nothing is really very frightening.

— Gertrude Stein

OVERCOMing ObSTACLES

Forget easy access. Think pilgrimage.

— M.C. Richards

*I*f you're anything like me, when faced with an obstacle, your first instinct is to walk, or run to somewhere else. Other tasks suddenly loom big in importance, like alphabetizing the spices... Once, when I was working on my first book, I actually found myself cleaning the oven—that's how much I wanted to avoid the task at hand. In that case, the problem was fear. It usually is.

One of the biggest obstacles to overcome in keeping a journal is the fear of someone finding it and reading it. This fear often stems from having had a diary found as a child and being punished or ridiculed for it. Or maybe a parent or teacher came to you out of concern over what you'd written in your journal. Whatever the particulars, your privacy may have been violated, and chances are, you stopped recording your thoughts altogether.

Here's what happened to me. In sixth grade, I kept what was meant to be an autograph book, and as I didn't run into movie stars or famous writers very often in suburban St. Louis, I kept it as a sort of diary: such and such happened at school today; I think Carol likes me; I'm mad at Paul. That sort of thing. One day, an older sister found the book and came to me, offering what she felt was good advice: "Don't write down anything you don't want people to know." I was on my way to summer camp in Michigan. She was afraid the other boys might find my notebook and make fun of me. That's when the diary stopped. I threw it away. What's more, I'd gotten the notion that this was yet something else that boys did not do, and I was ashamed.

It wasn't until seven years later that I started again. This time, I kept the notebooks in a metal strong box with a key to ensure privacy. This worked, because it enabled me to keep writing them, but I'd formed a habit of self-censoring that was so strong, I'm still amazed when I reread those volumes at what I didn't record about what was really going on.

I remember some years ago working with the wife of a political candidate who felt that everything she wrote down was likely to become public record, and so had a terrible time trying to keep a journal. In a way, she expressed fears we all have about our privacy, especially now. The challenge is this; to create a safe place for ourselves, a place where we can be alone with our own thoughts and feelings, no matter how messy they seem to us in the moment.

When I reread journals I kept 30 years ago, I'm struck by my language, which touches upon another obstacle to journal keeping; our relationship to our mother tongue or our second (or third) language, and our various experiences learning how to use that language in a formal and public way. The issue of language is further complicated by our ideas of who we are to ourselves and how we're related to the culture(s) we live in.

I was 18 when I started keeping journals again after my first experiment in sixth grade. I was entering college, hungry for the world of ideas and answers to my life. Part of my purpose in going to college was to expand my vocabulary in literary criticism, music theory, psychology, and art history. In order to learn the language of the academy, I imitated it in my essays, in conversation, in letters, and in my journal; and so those notebooks are full of awkward, stiff, formal prose.

Some years later, after I'd been living in England for a time, I'd adopted certain British idioms and spellings. In speaking, I'd softened my consonants and lengthened the vowels. This was conscious. I didn't want to be taken right off for an American, which had a lot to do with the shame many of us lived with during the Vietnam War. I was also trying to fit myself into a dominant culture, one I'd always suspected, as an English major, as being superior to my own. When I came to the end of my time overseas, I knew I had to come back to the States, to the American language as it was growing and changing. As a writer, I needed to come home.

As much as we use language to define ourselves and make ourselves known to others, we also use language to obscure ourselves, to keep us from being known. For the first 15 years I kept a regular journal, I was an active alcoholic. In addition to the language of academic discourse I'd learned in college, I was using language to keep myself from knowing too much about myself; it was a form of denial. And yet, as strong as that denial was, every once in a while, the psyche broke through to show a part of itself as a wound, a phobia, a terror, a deepening despair, and, of course—the alcoholic's specialty—self-pity. With all that, the journal helped keep me alive in those years. It was a place where I could speak myself into being, unfold myself with whatever language I had at hand, so that I had some presence in the world.

As a teacher, I've urged people to claim their own language and to find the urgency in what they have to say, so they'll insist on saying it clearly. Getting to this clarity is, more often than not, a messy process. It takes time, curiosity, and willingness. Clarity and power are more important than grammar and correctness. What counts in a journal is that the writing is clear to you. You must find a language in which you can be yourself to yourself; and then take it deeper, which often involves getting more specific about the senses and more honest about self-delusion.

If English is your second (or third) language, you might want to use a journal to stay in contact with your mother tongue; at the same time, you may want to use a journal to develop and expand your facility with English. The only diary my mother kept was written in French, in order to get regular practice using the language and to describe what she saw, felt, heard, and thought in the Paris of 1934.

Related to this discussion of language and identity is perfectionism, another obstacle that is connected to an ever-present sense of audience, a part of ourselves that is always reading over our shoulder. Even if we know our notebooks will never become public, we want to sound literate or intelligent and compassionate or hip; to ourselves, at least.

For this work, I suggest that you let go of everything you've learned about "style" or correctness. In this work, it's sometimes a great moment when syntax breaks down altogether and we write half-thoughts or phrases. For me this has often signaled some kind of breakthrough in understanding, some difficult truth surfacing despite my resistance.

For those of you who write in different dialects, I encourage you to explore them, make them do what you want them to do, say what you want them to say. No matter what the language, that's what we work with: what the language can and cannot express. French can say things that Russian can't. A line of Pablo Neruda's poetry can suddenly go flat in English.

When I taught at the Salt Institute for Documentary Studies here in Maine, I worked with a student from Chicago who was negotiating a contract with a large publisher. The book was about hip hop. She was a wonderful writer, full of juice and good humor and rapid-fire impressions of her world. When it came to the language of documentary, however, she struggled a great deal with her voice, which, by necessity, needed to be slower and more transparent to do her subject justice. Not that there's anything wrong with hip hop; it's just not effective when trying to give a sense of people's lives in the State of Maine.

In the end it was a question of how much range this writer wanted to have. Had I chosen to remain in the language of academic discourse, I could have never written the stories of my first book. I had to move into an entirely different mode of thought, the language of narrative, a language I'd rediscovered in my notebooks.

Another thing that has really held me back from journal keeping is whining. For years, it seems that's all I did—I could complain for pages and pages. In those days, the only time I went to the journal was when I felt bad. As a result, I ended up chronicling misery. Re-reading the entries was deadly. I bored myself stupid. I needed to widen my area of exploration, to pick up the journal not only in times of crisis or pain, but also when I felt OK.

Then there's the "every day" rule. That's what a journal is, isn't it? Something you write in every day. Many people claim they're not really doing it right unless they're making entries every day, and because that's an unreasonable goal for many people, they quit. Here's my suggestion; write in your notebook when the spirit moves you. I go days, sometimes weeks, without making an entry. The important thing is that I've created a place for me to go—a place that's quiet—a private place that's my own. I carry my journal with me everywhere, so I can write in it while

I'm waiting for my car's wheels to be aligned, or while my clothes are in the dryer at the laundromat, or in a restaurant if, say, someone has stood me up...

(Meanwhile, back at whining...)

Another obstacle is the notion that we don't have enough time—for anything, much less something as inessential as keeping a journal. I believe the inner life *is* essential, perhaps more essential to us now than at any other time in history, and journals help keep the inner life alive. Also, we tend to think we need big blocks of time without distraction, but who has that? All you need is about 20 minutes—that's enough time to make a drawing, record a dream, or solve a problem by working it out on paper. When you have longer periods of time, you can go deeper if you want to. Once you start making small amounts of time for yourself, you'll want to make more, so you will make more. And before you know it, you'll have some of those larger blocks of time you thought were impossible.

So we begin where we are. The important thing is to begin. And then continue. Not every day, but when the spirit moves, or the belly, or the heart. And not only when we're miserable, but also when we're wildly happy.

Today in my journal, I joke, I whine, I explore, I wrestle, I wound, I betray, I cavort, I seduce, I abandon,

I suffer, I heal, I celebrate, I tell lies. I lament. I justify. I trick myself and burst in upon new truths. My journal is a house, a Great Hall, a toxic waste dump, a temple, a gymnasium. My notebooks are full of cycles, circles, repetitions, spirals, jealousies, manias, dark thoughts, denials, obsessions, despair, self-pity. But also moments of insight and grace.

There are as many kinds of journals as people who keep them. Well, almost. Runners keep a runner's log, a kind of journal. Gardeners sometimes keep a notebook about what they plant and where and how everything is doing, as well as including thoughts about the garden, a kind of meditation. Elders often want to write down their memories for their children or grandchildren, and for this, they use a kind of journal. A baby book can be a journal. A travel journal allows people to record their thoughts, impressions, and details of places. So it's useful to get clear about what your intention is for keeping a journal, and to do this, you might want to come up with a working definition.

Exercise

Name the book you write in. What do you call it? If you were to tell someone you were keeping one, how would you refer to it? A journal? A diary? What's your definition? List ways in which you've used a personal notebook in the past.

Exercise

What would you like to see yourself do in this book? Maybe more of what you already do. Maybe something new. Make a list.

Exercise

Write down a few things you'd never dream of doing in your book.

Exercise

What do you notice about the parameters you've set for yourself? What rules do you have about keeping a journal? Which of these "rules" would you like to hang on to for the moment? Which ones (if any) are you willing to alter or let go?

What do I name the book I write in?

I think I've always called my journal a journal, never a diary. Now that I've said that, I wonder if it's true. Come to think of it, I may have called that first autograph book a diary in sixth grade. I think by the time I was 18, I was thinking of my notebooks as journals. I did go through a period of calling them daybooks, after *The Daybooks* of Edward Weston. And my definition of journal has changed, become less and less literary, more and more useful to me, something I can do anything in: write, draw, doodle, fill with newspaper clippings, collage.

What would I like to see myself do in this book?

> Be more honest.
> Take more time.
> Use more detail in descriptions of people, places, objects, events.

What parameters have I set for myself? Rules?

None that I can think of, except that I don't generally work on fiction or essays, writing that is for a public audience; though I have been known to make notes… which I promptly forget or can't find.

What would I never dream of doing in or with my journal?

I once worked with a woman who, when she finished a notebook, would burn it. I was horrified. She explained that her whole purpose for keeping a journal was to vent feelings, to get rid of them, so why would she want to keep the notebooks when they were full? She had a good point. Even so, I can't imagine burning my old journals, though there've been times I've wished I could. I also can't imagine ever doing algebra in my journals.

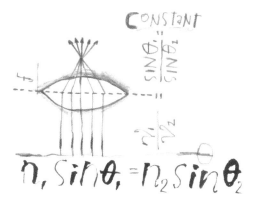

How about another kind of obstacle—those little voices in our heads that say, *Why bother? Who do you think you are? Your life isn't important enough to write down.* In the coaching profession, we call these gremlins, after Richard Carson's great book *Taming Your Gremlin.* Briefly defined, a gremlin is a thought form that holds us back from what we really want to do; an old idea or a fear, if you will.

One of my clients used to stop the car on her way to work, get out, open the back door, take her gremlin by the hand and walk it to the side of the road. "Gremlin Day Care," she called it. And she never bothered picking it up after work. Another client drew her gremlin as a dot on the corner of a piece of paper, tore it off, put it in her mouth, chewed until it was a good spit ball, stepped into her back yard, and spat. The point is, it's good to acknowledge that you've got an obstacle or a gremlin, or whatever you want to call it, and then get really physical and concrete about it. Use your imagination to handle it in such a way that allows you to get back to what you want to do—which just might be writing in your journal today.

Exercise

Describe one of your gremlins—in detail. List some of its favorite sayings/rules/laws/ideas about the world. Then find a creative way in which to deal with the gremlin. For example, it might need something of its own to do to let you get on with your day. Try a couple of these ideas until you find one that works for you.

Once a coaching client described her gremlin with such affection, I said, "It sounds adorable."

"Oh it is!" she said.

"What does it need in order to leave you alone?" I asked.

"A pair of Converse All Star high-topped sneakers," she said without hesitating. "Green ones. I'm going to go right out and buy a pair this afternoon."

She did just that. And it did the trick.

Exercise

Describe in great detail some obstacle you face. If it's a person, really go for it. Detail is what you're after. If it's something like lack of time, then try to personify it, give it a shape, a color, a texture, and smell. Now see if you can locate its gift, the way this obstacle serves you, or what it may be inviting you to learn.

Often when I've removed an obstacle, three more present themselves. Sometimes, I just have to sit with them for a time. While working on this chapter, for example, I was stuck for nearly a week. I avoided it. I did publicity for my workshops, I talked to prospective clients about coaching, and I planned the classes I was to teach at the art school for the upcoming term. I got *really* regular about going to the gym, and then I admitted I was stuck and started to get at what scared me. Not everybody was going to find this book useful. And I wanted to reach everyone. I'm also speaking as myself and not through the voice of a character. As a fiction writer, one of my last concerns in the writing process is the audience. Writing this book, I'm almost always aware of who I'm addressing.

I took a minute to write through this fear in my journal and then came to the desk to revise this chapter. That night I had a dream in which I was riding in a car with a man I didn't know, but whom I felt I could trust. He was driving along a ridge, through a forest, where there was no road. My sense was that we were driving down a peninsula because I could see water through the trees on my right. I felt good about trusting the man driving, and irritated that I didn't know where we were going.

So the obstacle was asking me to slow down and deepen my trust in the process.

DrEAMWoRK

Proceed from the dream outward.

— C.G. Jung

I know. Some of you are thinking: But I don't dream. Let's take a moment to consider this. According to most psychologists, we all dream. The question is whether or not we remember our dreams. Some of us feel we're dreaming all the time in some way, not just at night. And there are any number of ways of remembering night dreams. One woman I worked with used to set her alarm clock for 3:00 a.m. to interrupt her dream, so she could sit up and write the dream in a notebook she kept on her bedstead. Other people keep a notebook handy and wait until they wake up naturally. Still others ask the psyche for a dream before they go to sleep. Conventional wisdom says to tell (or write) your dream before breakfast or you will lose it.

If you are unable to capture your dreams, try noticing how you feel upon waking. Is there anything? A first thought? An image? A color? A sensation in the body? Write it down. This is a step toward access. It is important how we approach the unconscious. The psyche needs to know we are respectful and serious before she will let us glimpse her treasures.

But why bother about dreams anyway? First of all, they're a way in; dreams are one way the psyche has of making itself known to us, of bringing what's unconscious to consciousness. Working with dreams promotes greater awareness of our wholeness—how we are, where our bodies, minds, and emotions meet. Dreams point to where our deepest instincts and energies want to go. Whatever our beliefs, dreams provide us with one way of finding meaning in our lives. By paying close attention to what's going on in the depths, we can begin to modify our behavior in the world so we don't get sidetracked quite as often, or for as long, by irritation, anger, or fear. This connection to the unconscious allows us to more easily pull back our projections onto others, so we can maintain clearer relationships.

Let's say you've tried the notebook beside your bed. You've asked your psyche for your dreams, and nothing happened. You still don't remember your dreams. All right then, make one up. Write your fantasy in the present tense. Let your imagination lead you, no matter how silly or absurd it may seem. You can do all of the following dreamwork exercises on a fantasy and get fine results. Fantasies are full of information and can provide us with insight into what's going on beneath the surface.

Keep in mind that we're not looking to see how neurotic we are; we're not viewing dreams from a point of view of pathology. Instead, I invite you to be curious about what's in a dream or fantasy and get interested in how that might be of use to you.

Here's an example of a waking fantasy:

I am walking down a road, past a big old house covered with blossoming vines. The red front door is open. It's cool and dark inside. All the shutters are shut. I think about going in. It's a hot, bright day, and I'm thirsty, but I decide to keep walking. A porcupine squirms out from the foundation of the house, one of the basement windows, and runs across the lawn to the dirt road. I pass a tree with a large snake coiled around the lowest limb. I come to a crossroads, where there is a VW bug, a red one. I get in, start up the motor, and drive away on a paved road toward the East.

Full of surprising information for me, this fantasy is in many ways more intricate than the dream I reported to you in Chapter One. Anything that comes to mind will do. The first six of the following exercises come from the *Jungian-Senoi Dream Manual*, an extraordinary resource by Strephon Kaplan-Williams, published in 1983. Number seven came out of regular dialogue work we do in journal groups.

Exercise

1. Write out your dream or fantasy in the present tense, as I've done in the example above. Leave the facing page blank. If you need more than one page, leave all subsequent facing pages blank. In this way, you can work with the dream adjacent to the text, rather than pages later.

2. Next, give the dream a title—"War & Peace," "Bambi Meets Godzilla." What's the dream about? Write the title at the top of the blank page facing the text of your dream.

3. Take a minute to consider the dream's major themes (e.g., intimacy, the father story, competition, secrets, looking for home, relationship to the body). Write down the theme(s).

4. Make a list of feelings encountered in your dream (fear, anger, relief, joy). Note how you felt when you woke up, especially if it was different from the feelings in the dream.

5. What questions do you have of the dream? Do you have questions for characters in the dream? Write these questions down.

6. What question(s) does the dream seem to be asking of you?

7. Have a dialogue with the dream, or a character, animal, or object in the dream. This may sound odd, but try it anyway. Begin with one of the questions. Ask the dream something, and see how it responds.

You ask:
The dream says:
You say:

See where the conversation goes. Notice what you discover. Notice, for example, who has the last word. What do you know about the dream that you didn't know before?

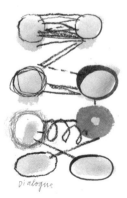

Dialogue

Let's take a closer look at my dream from the first chapter as an example:

I'm riding in a car with a man I don't know, but whom I feel I can trust. He drives along a ridge, through a forest, where there is no road. My sense is that we're driving down a peninsula, because I can see water through the trees on my right. I feel good about trusting the man driving and irritated that I don't know where we're going.

Title: The Driver

Theme: Trust, pleasure, faith, not knowing, travel.

Feelings: Trust, happiness, curiosity, irritation.

Questions: Who is driving?

How are we related to one another?

Where are we going?

When will we get there?

What kind of car are we in?

Are we in Maine?

How will we get back?

Can I, in fact, trust this guy?

Does he know where he's going?

Questions the dream seems to ask me:

> What are you afraid of?
> If you feel good about trusting, why not do it more often?
> Where do you want to go?
> What else about the ride are you enjoying?

Dialogue

Me: How will we get back?

Driver: I'm a man who's not concerned about getting anywhere. I like the going. I like driving. I'm a good driver, even if there isn't a road. I like the woods and water. I like movement. I enjoy your company.

Me: Thanks. Mostly I'm having a good time, but I'd like to know where we're going.

Driver: To the end of this path.

Me: What's there?

Driver: Dunno. Last time I came this way, there was a beach at the end of it. I drive this way because I'm curious. And I enjoy the scenery along the way.

Me: I wish I could be more like you.

Driver: What's stopping you? Would it help if you did the driving?

Me: No. Actually I like not driving; it gives me a chance to look around.

This is a good place to stop, though it could go on. What I notice is how much this feels to be a dream about revising this book, how I'm slowing down to discover new things. This makes me impatient because I've set a deadline for myself. I want to have this draft done by the time I leave for New Mexico in less than a month. The dream and the driver remind me that this could be about having fun, which was my original intent. In some ways, the book has become a lifeless chore. The dream reminds me that I'm curious and like seeing how things change in the process of revision. The dream also reminds me that I know where I'm going, or at least where I am in the moment, whether or not I reach the sea. The dream reminds me that keeping a journal is not about the destination or the product, that the pleasure is in the process of discovery, its unfolding. The dream reminds me to take my own advice: lighten up, trust the process, be willing to be surprised. Literally: enjoy the ride.

Here's an exercise I developed borrowing a technique called Percept Language, developed by John and Joyce Wier and continued by Alexandra Merrill. A friend suggested I try working with my dreams in this way, though Percept Language has many more applications and far-reaching powerful effects on all kinds of relationships. After each noun, write the words *part of me*. You can even try this after certain adjectives, depending upon where your mind leads you.

When I rewrite my waking fantasy, here's how it looks:

*I have me walking down a road **part of me** past a big old house **part of me**, covered with blossoming **parts of** a vine **part of me**. The red front door **part of me** is an open **part of me**. It's cool and dark on the inside **part of me**. All the shutter **parts of me** are shut. I think about going into this **part of me**. It's a hot, bright day **part of me**, and I am a thirsty **part of me**, but I decide to keep on walking. A porcupine **part of me** squirms out of the foundation **part of** the house **part of me**, one of the basement window **parts of me**, and runs across the lawn **part of me** to the dirt **part of** the road **part of me**. I pass a large **part of** the snake **part of me** coiled around the lowest **part of** the limb **part of me**. I come to a crossroads **part of me** and drive away on a paved **part of** the road **part of me** toward the East **part of me**.*

Notice how I insert **part of me** more often with some interesting results. Why would I insert **part of** between *large* and *snake*? Why not the *large snake* **part of me**? Instinct. A hunch. Do you feel the difference? This way, the *snake* part of me has more than one aspect to it. *Large* here might suggest something important. The *snake* **part of me** might be associated with the reptilian brain; a very old way of my knowing. Notice the difference between saying *the lowest limb* **part of me** and *the lowest* **part of the** *limb part of me*. A subtle difference, perhaps, but a difference nonetheless. Somehow, it suggests being closer to the ground.

The point is to find your own patterns of association. Working with dreams in this way locates all aspects of the dream within the dreamer.

IN MY DREAM I AM
PLAYING GUITAR ON A STAGE
WITH A HUGE AUDIENCE AND
I CANNOT PLAY ONE LICK
AWAKE OR ASLEEP

Exercise

Rewrite the text of your dream or fantasy and insert "part of me" after every noun and any modifiers you choose. Again, you may want to leave the right hand page blank for notes, associations, reflection, and new insights.

This is, of course, only one way to look at dreams. The idea is that everything in the dream belongs to the dreamer. Practitioners of Gestalt psychology work with dreams in a great way. One of the things they do is to tell the narrative of the dream from different points of view. In my fantasy, I might have the house tell the dream, or the porcupine, or the road, or the tree limb, or the snake, elaborating any associations that come to mind.

Exercise

Tell the dream from the point of view of another character, an animal, or an object in the dream. Try it more than once, from more than one perspective.

Exercise

Now try drawing the dream. If you're getting tired of the one you've been working on, switch to a new dream or fantasy. But how the hell do you draw a dream? That was my question. I was teaching a workshop once and we'd just done a dream exercise. I asked the group if anyone had other ways of working with dreams.

"I often draw mine," said one woman.

"Oh yes," I said, "what a good idea. I don't because, of course, I can't draw."

The woman sat straight up.

"Don't be silly. Everyone can draw," she insisted.

So we tried it. I drew the characters in my dream as stick figures in a cartoon storyboard to show the passing of time and to delineate different scenes. Some drew their dreams in a more abstract way. Then we all wrote about what we saw in our drawings. That a monster is smaller than a lamp, for example, is not necessarily an indication of poor hand/eye coordination. It might show the importance we give at the moment, say, to the lamp; a source of light, versus the monster; something we may associate with darkness.

DRAWing

Paint as you like and die happy.

— Henry Miller

emember when I told that group I couldn't draw? It was a lie. I knew that, and yet a part of me must have believed it because I said it. I hear myself say things like that all the time. Who knows why? What matters is that the notion I can't draw has not stopped me from filling all kinds of notebooks with doodles, designs—in fact, drawing. I even go to drawing groups from time to time with my pad of newsprint and a bundle of charcoal. I've done this all my life, but I tell myself I'm no good at it. A gremlin. Who cares? The point is, I keep doing it.

I mention this because I think many of us have blocks about drawing similar to those we encounter when we sit down to write. Somewhere along the line, someone may have told us we couldn't draw well, or we saw quite plainly that what we drew didn't look a thing like what we were trying to draw, or we saw for sure ours wasn't what the kid next to us was drawing, so many of us stopped altogether.

After my first book was published, without quite knowing why, I got hungry to do things I knew nothing about. I started to study ecstatic dancing. I signed up for a night school painting class. On the first evening, the teacher told us about the toxicity of oil paint. "So we're not supposed to eat them," I said. She suggested which solvent to use, told us how linseed oil worked, and how to clean up. Then she told us to mix our palettes. I wasn't even sure how to get the tubes of paint open, much less how to mix a palette, so I stared at the woman to my right, who seemed to know just what to do. My point is, I was in a state of not-knowing, what the Buddhists call "beginner's mind," what I prefer to think of as original incompetence. I was curious and excited. I was playing around, eager to see what would happen next.

One night a few years ago in a painting class, we were working from the figure. On a break, the model walked around in her robe, looking at our work. One painter said she hadn't done any justice to the model's lovely red hair. Another apologized for making the model look fat.

"Oh, don't worry," said the model. "I never take any of this personally."

When she came to my easel, she leaned over and whispered, "Change those eyes before the end of class, or I'll break your knees."

She had a legitimate gripe. The figure I'd painted looked demented. I don't know how to paint eyes.

When I draw from the figure, more often than not, I make it look as though the model has been in a bad accident; everything seems dislocated. I lose all sense that there's a skeleton beneath the musculature. Even when I remember to measure the distance between knee and foot, and check the angle of the hip and shoulder, the drawing looks all golly-wompus and distorted. As I look deeper, I begin to see how the body fits together. Rendering it is another story.

I keep drawing because I'm curious about what I will see and how I will see it. Drawing becomes an exploration, a process I enter. What I'm waiting for is a moment of seeing, the *feeling* of seeing. It's tough to describe, and it has nothing really to do with what's on the page in front of me. It's what I see in the object or body itself, a kind of radiance, a glimpse into the life inside.

It's not that I don't value craft. I teach at an art school. I admire a thing that's well made, whether it's a table, a pot, a painting, or an essay. Drawing images in my journal is purely about the process, never about a product, though there's value in keeping sketchbooks with it in mind to show, or even sell the drawings. That's not, I think, the best use of drawing in a personal notebook. Here, craft can prevent us from doing it. Better to approach drawing in this context with curiosity, with a sense of play.

When we draw, we explore another kind of language, one with its own sort of grammar and syntax. Visual language makes meaning in ways that are markedly different from the language of words. We do not tend to read visual language from left to right, at least not consciously. Visual language

isn't experienced in time the same way as words and sentences. Visual language does not often suggest a narrative, much less an argument, though there are exceptions. Because our culture relies most heavily on the language of words, visual language can feel foreign and intimidating. Understandably, many of us hesitate to try out a new language. We refuse to draw, and this limits our range of expression.

Say you wake up one morning and sit with a cup of coffee or tea, ready to take up your journal. But there's no dream to record, and nothing much happened the day before that you want to write about.

Now what? I myself am a word man, a writer. I'm forever remaking the world into phrases, paragraphs, and stories. I'm also aware of images from dreams, memories, and fantasies that remain in my mind most clearly as pictures. Try as I might, I can't quite get them into words as powerfully as they remain as images in my head.

Exercise

Draw how you're feeling. Let your pen or pencil move across the page without much thought. This can be as abstract or concrete as you please. Again, as with dreams, you might want to use the left hand page, leaving the right hand page blank so you can write about what you see in the drawing, or write a dialogue with the drawing, or make another drawing in answer to the first.

Exercise

Draw your boredom. What do you notice? Make some notes on the opposite page. In what ways does this drawing interest you? What interests you about your boredom? What makes you curious?

Exercise

A big long list of things to DRAW:

- Your wild excitement

- Your sense of expectation

- The anxiety about what you face at work

- The good fortune you anticipate

- The joy in your belly

- Your horniness

- Yourself at the age when you felt most powerful

- Yourself when you felt most vulnerable

- Your worst fear

- Your greatest hope

- Your full body—where it is tight and aches, where it is getting stronger and healing, where it is most flexible

- Your anger, happiness, or sadness

- Animals you know

- Exotic animals

- The animals you are

- Your heart—physical and emotional

- A problem

- A solution

- A source of energy; that part of you or
  your life that needs energy; then a way
  to connect them

- Your garden

- Your kitchen

- Your faith

- Your erotic fantasies; a whole series of
  erotic drawings

DiALOGUES

Because inside human beings
is where God learns.

— Rainer Maria Rilke

translated by
Robert Bly

W e have dialogues all the time, even when we're not talking. Getting ready to write this chapter, I sat here at the desk and heard the following inside my head:

> —Should I go to the post office now, or wait till after lunch?
> —After lunch…
> —But if I go now, I'll be able to run the other errands I have on the way home…
> —The mail won't have come yet; wait until you've had lunch…
> —I don't want to interrupt myself this afternoon; I want to finish this chapter on dialogues. I can wait till tomorrow to check the mail…
> —But what if something important is in my mailbox?

The dialogue as a teaching tool goes back at least as far as Socrates. Ira Progoff discusses it at length in *At a Journal Workshop*. The granddaddy of Gestalt psychology, Fritz Perls, was famous for his use of dialogue. He'd have his clients imagine whomever they needed to talk to (including themselves) seated in an empty chair, and then have a conversation.

Like drawing, dialogues have a wide range of uses. Dialogues found their way into my workshops through what I now call the Monster Exercise. For a long time, I referred to this exercise as Cleaning Out the Basement. First we drew our least favorite aspect of ourselves, then described its life: what it ate, its habits, where it lived, and who its friends were. Once we'd gotten acquainted, we wrote a dialogue with this least favorite part of ourselves. We discovered that it had lots to say to us, and, more often than not, we had more compassion for it after engaging it in conversation. Some people felt empowered, having given this part of themselves a piece of their mind.

I'm not sure how this evolved into the Monster Exercise, but I think a therapist friend had something to do with it. She once described how she worked with children's fear. She'd get kids to draw the monsters they imagined in order to externalize them—not to dismiss or negate them, but to take a look at them, and literally get bigger than the monsters.

Robert Johnson or Marion Woodman—I can't remember which—tells a story about Jung's collaborator, Marie Louise von Franz and her demons. One day she was working on an article or a book, and her demon voice started up: "You're wasting your time. Who do you think you are? You don't know what you're doing." That sort of thing. It's astonishing to me that after a lifetime of distinguished accomplishment, von Franz was still troubled by nasty voices—but she was.

She stopped writing, went to her filing cabinet, pulled out a favorable review of her most recent book, and read it out loud to the pests. When she had finished, they said, "Yeah, but that's an American review; they always love your work." So she went back to her filing cabinet, pulled out another review, and read it to them in German. Then she could get back to work.

The point is, she took them seriously and read to them out loud. Something about voicing one's response to monsters is very powerful. Notice that she didn't just ignore them. Neither did she try to slay them. Her feeling was that you can't kill your demons; you can only educate them. When we take the time to communicate with these inner figures, we often find them to be frightened and needy. Sometimes they tell us what they need, and if we can give it to them, as I pointed out with gremlins, they go back to sleep and leave us alone.

And monsters are not always called for. Once, I was teaching a journal group at the Portland Public Library, and I introduced the Monster Exercise. I expected everyone to get out colored pencils or markers and get on with it. I was in fact, ready to draw my own, when I heard a loud noise. A woman at the other end of the seminar table slammed her palm down and said, "No! I'm not drawing another f---ing monster. I'm sick of them." I blinked. There was no urging her gently into trying the exercise. She was adamant.

"All right, then," I said. "Draw one of your angels." And so she did. She drew one of her angels and described its diet, its habits, and habitat. Then she wrote a dialogue.

"That was much better," she said afterwards.

I began using the Angel Exercise, sometimes as an alternative to the Monster and sometimes separately. I was all set to give the Angel Exercise to a group of fourth graders one day, when the teacher said, "No."

"Why not?" I said.

"It's religious," she said.

"What's religious?" I said.

"Angels," she said. "They're religious. This is a public school. We can't do it."

So we did monsters, instead.

Monster Exercise

1. Begin by drawing one of your monsters. Not a person you know and not a Hollywood monster, but one of your own. This might be a bad habit, a craving, a pattern of negative thought, or a resentment. Or just start drawing any old monster. It can be as abstract or as representational as you please. Include details.

2. Name this monster. Now write a profile. What does it eat? Where does it live? (Not just "inside me", where in you? Be specific). Or, In a cave? By a waterfall? In a swamp? Describe its habitat, its daily comings and goings. Who does it hang around with? Does it stay alone? What are its favorite colors? Where does it shop? Where does it go on vacation? Does it take vacations? What was its most embarrassing moment? Refer back to your drawing if you feel stuck.

3. Write a dialogue. Again, you might begin with a question to get the conversation going. Imagine how it would communicate with you, and describe that. Let the conversation go on for as long as you need to. Then go back and see what you notice. What did you learn? It's always interesting, for example, to see who has the last word.

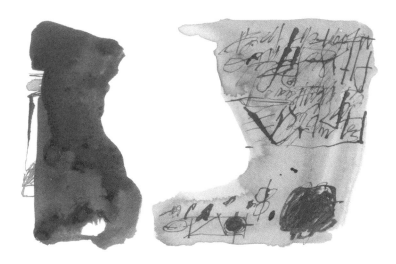

Exercise

Try writing a dialogue with…

- Your body
- Your heart
- Your past
- Your future
- Your faith
- God
- Friends
- Family
- Lovers
- Pets

- Animals inside you, the animals you are
- Totems
- Guides
- An injury or wound
- Your healing process
- A substance you struggle with
- Plants
- Trees
- Clouds
- The wind
- Your garden
- The sun
- The moon
- Planets
- Your rising sign
- Historical figures
- Mythological figures such as: Zeus, Aphrodite, Pan, Athena, Dionysius, Artemis, Persephone, Aries, Hephaestus...

UNSENT LETTERS: Monologues

This is my letter to the World
That never wrote to Me —

— Emily Dickinson

*I*n the age of e-mail, we tend to forget the power of letters. I'm thinking here of letters too important to be entrusted to the authorities; letters carried across borders and delivered by hand; love letters; letters that never arrived; letters that crossed in the mail; letters discovered by the wrong person; letters that changed the course of history. I'm thinking of the insight we get into the great anarchist, Emma Goldman, by reading her love letters, or the letters of Vanessa Bell to her sister, Virginia Woolf. It wasn't until I read Flannery O'Connor's letters that I could ever fully enter her fiction.

Letters are focused, intimate, direct, and powerful. Letters have to do with longing and proclaiming, rejoicing, consoling, lamenting and blaming.

I discovered the value of unsent letters when I was having a fight with a friend who had cancer, and I needed to clarify my feelings. I was exhausted and angry. I'd given this friend an enormous amount of time and energy, and here we were in conflict. Someone suggested I write a letter to my friend every day for the next five days—not to send, but to explore my feelings. I could be as honest as I needed to be, as impolite, as inappropriate as I pleased. I was free to contradict myself and to be unfair. That's exactly what I did in my journal each day for the next five days: ranted, raved, wailed, whined, grieved, raged, accused, defended myself, attacked, and rationalized. At the end of the week, I felt ready to write my real response, the letter I would actually send. It ended up being less than a page, reaffirming my love for her and my regard for our friendship. I also set some clear boundaries.

Though it was not a letter intended to end our friendship, I never heard from her again. The point is, I got clear about what I needed to say without emotional hooks or any hidden agenda. What I discovered was what I had begun to suspect; that one of the unspoken rules of our friendship was that I wasn't allowed to have appropriate boundaries. Unspoken and entirely unconscious, the agreement affirmed that due to her terminal illness, my friend was completely in charge; whatever she wanted, she got.

I tell this story here to point out the power of the unsent letter to move one to greater clarity. Once clear in my own mind and heart, I knew how to act without regard to the outcome, though I'd expected and hoped for something different. I came to accept that what happened was exactly right for both of us, though painful at the time. I honestly believe that there was no love lost between us; in fact, our silence in her last year taught me a great deal about the power of loving through disharmony and discord. It taught me something about the power of prayer and surrender and forgiveness. I can't say what my friend learned, but I can say that these unsent letters led me to one of the most profound healing experiences of my life.

The journal itself might be considered to be a letter. Anaïs Nin's famous diaries began as letters to her father. More often, though, a journal is a letter to ourselves. Consider, then, the uses of a letter we write with someone else in mind, but which we hold onto. You might write to anyone: figures from history or fiction, someone you're mad at or in love with, even someone who is dead.

Exercise

Write an unsent letter, or a series of unsent
letters over time to:

- Someone with whom you're angry
- Someone you've hurt
- Someone you're in love with
- Your future self
- The boy or girl you were
- A dead friend or relative
- An author
- Someone who's hurt you
- Socrates
- Sappho
- Your boss
- Your boss's supervisor
- The boss of your boss's supervisor
- The President of the United States of America
- An artist whose work you love
- An artist whose work you hate
- A public figure you admire or despise
- Your pet(s), or other animals you can think of
- God
- Angels

25
Places
I want
to go: northern
Minnesota
Tibet Fiji Saskatchawan
Iowa Vancouver IdaHO
alaska Montana Turkey
Iceland Tetons
New Orleans Japan
NEW ZEALAND

Lists

When in doubt, make a list.

— My Mother

I was never much of a list maker. When I did make a list, I'd usually lose it. A couple of things changed my opinion of lists (and list makers). The first was a friend who, when he made one, put "make a list" at the top of it, so he could cross something off as soon as he finished making the list. He said this gave him some momentum. A book I read some years ago expanded my notion of list making in wonderful ways. I believe it was called *The 59¢ Therapist*, and I've tried everywhere to locate it with no luck. This book made me see that lists can do a lot more than remind us what we have to pick up at the store. The author suggests making lists of 100 items. That sounds like a lot, but here are some tips: write fast, feel free to repeat, and don't think too much.

Here's one of my lists as an example:

Alfred's List of Things to Let Go Of

1. Fear
2. Obsession with M.
3. Pain
4. Shoulder pain
5. Too much responsibility
6. Fear of lack of money
7. Fear of violence
8. Fear of car trouble
9. Fear of death
10. Worry
11. Distraction
12. Shame
13. Fear of solitude
14. Self-criticism
15. Loneliness
16. Feeling apart
17. Failure
18. Outsider feeling
19. Self-righteousness
20. Despair
21. Depression
22. Self-pity
23. I'm not good enough
24. People don't like me
25. Something's wrong with me

26. I don't fit
27. I'm superior
28. I don't fit in
29. Why am I alone?
30. Why does no one hear me?
31. Why does no one see me?
32. Why does everyone always choose someone else?
33. Not me
34. Always
35. Never
36. Blame
37. Shame
38. Fear of success
39. Fear of intimacy
40. Wishy washy
41. Wimpiness
42. Cowardice
43. Laziness
44. Paralysis
45. Fear
46. Dread
47. Blame
48. Shame
49. Fear
50. Pettiness
51. Irritation
52. Focus on others

53. Who's following the rules
54. Who's not
55. I'm not OK
56. I'll always be alone
57. Something's wrong with me
58. Damaged beyond repair
59. I don't want intimacy
60. Fear of being seen
61. Fear of being heard
62. Fear of attention
63. Blame
64. Resentment
65. Hate
66. Jealousy
67. Everybody's happy but me
68. Everybody's got it but me
69. Fear
70. Scarcity
71. Pettiness
72. Meanness of spirit
73. Gossip
74. Vindictiveness
75. Control
76. Judgements
77. Negativity
78. Criticism
79. Self-hate

80. Fear
81. Coffee (no way!)
82. Sugar (no way!)
83. Loneliness
84. Fear
85. Concepts
86. Old ideas
87. Worry
88. I don't want intimacy
89. If I'm intimate, I cease to exist
90. Intimacy as annihilation
91. Fear
92. Resentment
93. False pride
94. Stupid judgments
95. Fear
96. Blame
97. Attachment
98. Jealousy
99. Spite
100. Pickiness

First, I made the list, repeating freely. One of the great things about list making is that it often generates its own momentum. On this particular day, I was eager to let go of a lot.

Then I went through the list and looked for patterns—one of the benefits of repetition. I underlined everything having to do with fear in one color, shame in another color, blame in another and so on. I often draw lines between items which seem related and find other colors to mark subsets that seem to be emerging.

One thing I noticed was, I got to "jealousy" toward the end of the list. This was clearly not something in the front of my mind, though this item has a particular charge to it. So I might want to write more about what jealousy is and why I want to let it go. What are my stories of jealousy?

All this has to do with noticing. That's all; awareness. In making the list, I felt myself letting go of some of the fear and the shame right then and there—at least for a time. I don't know about you, but I need practice. I need to know what "letting go" feels like; otherwise, it's too abstract, too theoretical.

I remember when I first heard people talk about "letting go"—and it seemed that's all anyone talked about for a number of years—I didn't get it. I had no idea. "Just let it go," everyone said. "How?" I asked. "What do you do?" Then a friend handed me a tennis ball. "Turn your hand over," he said. "Now open your fingers and let the ball drop."

Profound, eh? You might laugh, but this is how I began to get it—on the physical level. Letting go. Letting it drop. Or, as the old spirituals urge us, lay it down. A burden, a heavy load. Lay it on down.

I wasn't surprised that fear, shame and blame appeared so many times on my list, but I noticed a lot about their context and some of the specific things that still scare me. I noticed that coffee and sugar appeared with question marks and outright refusals, so I guess that I wasn't so serious about letting them go. In fact, a mug of hot coffee with honey is next to me as I type this. I learned something about letting go even in the process of making the list; the process of externalizing, of emptying my thought onto the page, which, in itself, was a sort of letting go. I still have trouble with it, and I still need practice. Listing 100 things to let go of continues to be useful to me.

What about a list of 100 *ways* of letting go?

I think I'll try it.

As with the other exercises you've tried, let these lists take you where they take you. Use your imagination and invent extensions, expansions, new exercises. But where to start?

Exercise

Make a list of lists you'd like to have, then take one of those ideas and make a list of 100 items. Use colored pencils or markers to underline repetitions and patterns. Write about what you learn—see where it leads you. Here's a list of possible lists you may not have thought of...

1. Ways of letting go
2. Fools I'll never have to suffer again
3. Gifts of my last trip to
4. Responsibilities I can shirk
5. Places I'd like to travel to
6. Feelings I would like to honor
7. Ways the body sounds
8. Things I love about my body
9. Things I love about my lover's body
10. Things that are hard to love about my lover
11. Things that are hard to love about my friend
12. Things that are hard to love about a family member
13. Gifts my father gave me
14. Gifts my mother gave me
15. Gifts my grandmother gave me
16. Gifts my grandfather gave me
17. Gifts my brother gave me
18. Gifts my sister gave me
19. Ways to manifest my intent
20. Ways to get out of my own way

21. Mad and foolish ideas
22. Useless regrets
23. Ways to expand my life
24. Things I'm good at
25. Ways to improve the quality of life at my work
26. Ways to improve my life at home
27. Ways to improve my erotic life
28. Affirmations
29. Promises I want to keep to others
30. Promises I want to keep to myself
31. Hard things I'd like to tell a loved one
32. Easy things I'd like to tell a loved one
33. People who've wounded me
34. People I've hurt
35. Things I'll never have to eat again
36. Fears that no longer plague me
37. Things I love to eat
38. Things I'd like to see myself do in my journal
39. Things I'd never dream of doing in or with my journal
40. Things I know
41. Things I don't know
42. Things I think I know, but really don't
43. Things I think I don't know, but really do
44. Things I know I don't know
45. Things I'd like to know more about
46. Things my father never told me
47. Things my mother never told me
48. Secrets

49. Lies
50. Wishes
51. Visions
52. Favorite sexual fantasies
53. Betrayals
54. Ways in which I've betrayed others
55. Things I forgive myself for
56. Things I forgive others for
57. Things I'm not ready to let go of yet
58. Ways in which I show myself I love myself
59. Ways in which I show others I love them
60. Ways of letting go of self-hate
61. Addictions
62. Ways to recover from addiction
63. Truths
64. Illusions
65. Ways to take care of my body
66. Animals I've loved
67. Animals I've feared
68. Things I never told my father
69. Things I never told my mother
70. Things that I wanted to do
71. Things that I'm glad I never did
72. Things to take with me
73. Things to leave behind
74. People I'd love to kiss
75. Cures for a headache
76. Cures for hiccoughs
77. Cures for cramps

78. Cures for the blues
79. Ancestors
80. Paintings I want to make
81. Stories I want to tell
82. Sculptures I want to make
83. Books I want to read
84. People who love me
85. Sources of money
86. People/groups I want to support
87. Men to dance with
88. Women to dance with
89. Steps to a more prosperous life
90. Ways of deepening my spiritual life
91. Ways to pray
92. Ways to be in touch with my guidance
93. Ways to follow the guidance I receive
94. People whose wisdom I trust
95. Ways in which I trust and use my intuition
96. Ways in which I know the Divine is working in my life
97. People to pray with
98. People to pray for
99. Ways to celebrate my sexuality
100. Messages from my soul.

All right, so you make a list, you repeat things, you underline in different colors. You notice what you notice. Now what?

Try writing about what you notice after you've made and color-coded your list. What, if anything, did you learn? What physical sensations did you have while making the list? What occurred to you? What made you curious? What did you discover? What did you already know? When you look at your lists, where do your thoughts take you?

Exercise

Now it's your turn. Take it from here and see where it leads.

1. WAYS of LEttiNg Go
2. FooLS I'll hEVEr have to SuFFEr AGain
3. Gifts FroM MY Last trip to
4. RESPONSiBiLitiEs I CAN SHiRK.
5. PLacES I'D LiKE to Travel To
6. FEELings I WouLD LikE to Honor
7. ways
8.
9.
10.
11.
12.

Problem Solving

Sometimes I go about pitying myself, and all the time
I am being carried on great winds across the sky.

— Chippewa saying

S ome years ago, I thought I was about done with college teaching—I'd had it. I was burned out. My students were lazy and hostile. I'd done everything I could to please them, and still they complained. I dreaded going into the classroom each week, and I grew more and more critical and short-tempered. What troubled me most is that I had loved teaching, devoted my life to it for some 20 years. Everything I tried to do to rectify the situations in class backfired and only made things worse. It was a nightmare, as if my evil twin had taken over. I was, in fact, in the grip of my shadow. In short, I was thoroughly miserable —and it was everybody else's fault.

So, I hired a life coach. I was ready to make some changes, and the changes I was most ready to make were in my approach to teaching. I wanted to get back to what I loved about teaching, the excitement, the surprise, bearing witness to my students' bravery as they struggled to make language express the truths they were discovering about themselves and literature and the world around them. In three months of working with my coach, Harry Faddis, I got back to what I valued most about teaching, and taught once again from that place in me; curiosity, enthusiasm, excitement. In other words, I changed myself, where I stood, how I perceived the situation, and then everything I did had a different sort of impact.

My students began to take bigger risks because they felt safe. They learned more, went deeper. Because I was able to listen to them, they listened to each other, felt connected, made community. At the end of their freshman year of art school, some said the class had helped them grow up. They were proud of what they accomplished, and I was delighted.

About eight months after I started working with Harry, I started coaches' training because I thought it would help my teaching even more. It did. And in the process, people started hiring me as their coach. In May of 2001, I passed my exam and became a Certified Professional Co-Active Coach. I tell this story not only to emphasize the power of changing my perspective, but also to underscore the importance of honoring my values. I had to get clear about what was most important to me and teach from that. Next I had to live from that. As my great colleague, visionary feminist Elly Haney used to say, "Live your values." It's a radical act. Think about it. Better yet, start doing it.

I developed the following exercises after a one-day journal workshop I taught at the Maine Writers and Publishers Alliance. I had a group that took off and flew from the very first exercise. We spent the whole day in the realm of metaphor and archetype, dreamscape, memory, and insight. I was thrilled. It was just that kind of group—except for one lady. At the end of the day, as others were handing back their evaluation forms, she complained that there'd been nothing much in the workshop for her. She'd wanted practical things to do in her journal, not all this fantasy stuff. I felt bad and wished she had spoken up earlier. I'd been swayed by the majority and ignored this one woman whose needs were markedly different. I even had one or two practical exercises on the list, which I'd skipped because we were having so much fun dreaming.

I learned something that day. At the beginning of a class, I have to get an idea why people are there, and then give exercises to meet a wide range of needs. I've come to value the necessity for practical problem solving, more and more. Middle age, I suppose. Whatever it is, I'm grateful. So here are some exercises in various forms of problem solving.

Exercise

1. Think of a goal you have, something you want to accomplish or acquire, a state of mind you'd like to reach. Maybe it's a long-range goal, maybe short-range. Write it down.

2. Now make a list of all the obstacles you can think of, everything that stands in the way of you reaching that goal. Big, small, any size or shape you can think of. Keep writing until you run out. (If you don't feel you have enough, call me, I'll lend you some of mine.)

3. Take a breath. Settle in and start writing about what your life would be without obstacles— without any at all. Not one. Use your imagination. Fantasize.

4. Take a moment to note how that felt to you, to imagine your life without obstacles. What did you learn?

5. Take another look at that list of obstacles. Which ones can you realistically alter or move beyond? And which ones still seem immutable? In other words, reassess the size and importance of these obstacles one by one. Take a minute to write about what you noticed.

The first time I did the above exercise with a group, I actually got frightened. I'd grown so accustomed to obstacles as something to push against and define myself by, I felt lost. How could I navigate without the big rocks in the harbor? My father came to mind. Using him as a sort of navigational tool, I invented my life largely in opposition to his. When he died, I had the same sort of fear I had doing this exercise the first time. How would I know what was right for me if my father wasn't around to disapprove? Happily, I had a number of people in my life who filled that role; silent and not-so-silent disapprovers, and of course I recruited some more. The next step was to let go of my need for opposition and to get a better compass, an inner one. I also needed new friends and lovers, people who were thrilled about what I was doing, who said, "Yes! Wonderful. Go for it."

Often, when faced with a challenge, we believe we're not up to it. In fact, nine times out of ten, that's the problem itself; our idea that we can't solve it. First we tell ourselves we don't have the time or resources. Then we shift deeper and tell ourselves we lack a particular quality needed to solve the problem; courage or generosity or patience or perseverance or the ability to forgive. So here's what we can do:

Exercise

1. Name a problem and write it down.

2. Think of a quality you'd need more of in order to solve the problem or meet the challenge. Focus on a quality in your character, not money or anything similarly external. Write down a few, choose one, and write for 10 or 20 minutes about what it would be like if you had more of this quality. For example: *With more patience, I could...* Or, *Now that I have the courage I need, I can...*

If the problem is about getting to something you want to do or make, then deadlines are most useful. In my life, they've become essential. When I was younger, I viewed deadlines as a sort of curse: they were almost always imposed from the outside. Some still are: my mortgage is due on the first of the month; I have to turn in grades at the end of each semester by a certain date. When I write fiction, however, I like to work without any idea of what a story is about, much less deadlines. This is especially true at the beginning of a project, but there does come a time when I need to think about finishing, and if it weren't for the deadlines I set last summer with my coach Harry, I'd have never finished the novella I started in 1995. I'd have never found a typist or hired my friend Karla to edit the manuscript or had it in Karla's hands in early August, so she could get it to a friend of hers in New York, from whom I'm still waiting to hear, but I'm talking about my deadlines, not someone else's.

I've developed a great respect for the power of deadlines. I've found that when setting deadlines, it's important to be both firm and flexible. I've also discovered that it helps a great deal if there's someone in your life holding you accountable for your deadlines. To be useful, a deadline must be more than a wish; "I'd like to finish that project in a couple of weeks," just doesn't have the clout we need. When you set a deadline, be specific about the goal and precise about the time; "I'll complete the project, including the charts, by next weekend." Don't set up unrealistic expectations, but don't let yourself off the hook either.

Once you have a deadline, it will be easier to map out the steps that will get you there. If your deadline is a month away, in two weeks you should be half done. One of my jobs is writing, and I schedule writing time for myself by drawing blocks of time in my day book—in ink. I make these appointments with myself and keep them because I know that without this discipline, I won't meet my deadline.

Exercises

1. Before you do anything else, decide what's important to you about the project you're considering. It could be anything: a series of paintings, a new front porch, getting into a relationship. Make a list of everything you can think of that you love about this project; what it will give you—the process. For example, what I love about writing is sound, heart, discovery, surprise, magic, spirit, humor, beauty, and connection.

2. Give yourself a deadline for a project you have in mind.

3. Then work backwards, breaking the process down into steps. What do you need to do just before completion, and just before that and before that? Allow enough time for each step and set target dates.

4. As you work toward them, allow yourself to alter the deadlines (you may be ahead of schedule), but only if you're making an honest effort to meet them. If you find you're not doing much at all on the project, ask yourself how important it is to you. Be honest—maybe it's something you don't need to do at all. If that's the case, forget it and move on to something else.

Goal _____

                                    Completion Date

Steps   1. _____   _____

  2. _____   _____

  3. _____   _____

  4. _____   _____

  5. _____   _____

  6. _____   _____

  7. _____   _____

  8. _____   _____

  9. _____   _____

  10. _____   _____

Accountability Buddy: _____

How often do you agree to contact this person to report on your progress until the project is complete or abandoned?

Let's say you have a problem making decisions. You go back and forth. Should I or shouldn't I? Maybe you should call a psychic. Good idea. Seriously. Some of my best friends work in that field, and they're good, always handy when a tough choice looms on the horizon. But let's say the psychic's phone is busy and you can't wait.

Exercise

Write down a choice that you're facing. Imagine you've made choice A. Write a journal entry dated six weeks ahead. Write for as long as you like about the life you imagine for yourself after you've made choice A. Then try the same thing with choice B. And so on. See what you notice.

Decisions, problems, and obstacles are all good things to address head on. Now what about an exercise that doesn't seem to be about problem solving directly, but that shifts our point of view? When I'm in the midst of a problem, I often need help getting unstuck, and this almost always involves changing my point of view.

Exercise

Make a list of 25 things you love to do; not things you love, but things you love to do. That's right, 25. If you can't think of 25 things you love to do—think harder.

Take a moment to review your list. What do you notice? Any surprises? What are they? Now try the following:

1. Write a "P" beside everything on the list you like to do with other people.

2. Write an "A" beside everything in the list you generally like to do alone. Some items will have an "A" and a "P."

3. Now draw a "$" beside everything on the list that requires money every time you do it.

4. Next, write "NP" alongside each item that needs planning in order to do it.

5. Then put an "S" beside anything you tend to do spontaneously.

6. Now put an "M" beside each thing you've done in the last month.

7. And a "W" beside everything on the list you've done in the last week.

8. Sit back and review your list. What do you notice about it now? Take some time to write down your impressions.

You may have noticed that you're doing more of the things you love to do more often than you'd thought. You may have discovered a greater number of things that you love to do which don't cost you money. You may have already thought of a way to do the simpler things you love to do more often in the coming days. All too often, we get so focused on a problem we're trying to solve that we lose sight of how much our present lives are already satisfying.

Exercise

In that same spirit, here's one based on the title of Zora Neale Hurston's autobiography: *I Love Myself When I'm Laughing… And Then Again When I Am Looking Mean and Impressive*. At the top of the page write: "I love myself when I am_____" and then fill in the rest. Make a list, or write a paragraph repeating "I love myself when I'm…" again and again. Let yourself go on and on. Really let yourself know something about yourself. Notice yourself loving yourself. If this feels slightly wicked and vainglorious, just shrug and keep writing. Surprise yourself by how often you love yourself when you are… simply because you are… being yourself, doing what you love yourself for doing.

MAPS and WILDERNESS

Cartographers are like angels,
they imagine everything
from the air.

— Elizabeth Knox

I know a woman whose sister once called the automobile club for directions from one end of Baltimore to the other. My friend knew I'd appreciate this because I have a sketchy sense of direction, at best. I once got lost in an airport that only had three gates. Growing up in St. Louis, I remember my father always told us that toward the Mississippi River was east; away from the river was west. If the river was to your right, you were facing north, and if it was to your left, you were headed south. Even so, I managed to get lost all the time.

A number of my friends and neighbors in Maine are astonished each year that I drive to New Mexico and back and don't end up in Canada; though once driving from Oklahoma City to St. Louis, I took a wrong turn and didn't realize until I'd nearly reached Manhattan (Kansas, not the other one) that I was heading west instead of east.

No doubt about it, maps come in handy; on road trips or walking around the center of a new city, or on a scavenger hunt. I have a drawer full of maps of bus routes in Amsterdam, London, Leningrad, Warsaw, and Beloit, Wisconsin. You never know when you might need one.

And what about other kinds of maps? The map of your creative life? A map of your heart? The map *to* your heart? Your career path as a kind of map. The jobs you've had. A map to your buried treasure.

Exercise

Make a list of the maps you wish you had (or maps you wish you'd had growing up). What might these be? Make the list as long as you want. Write fast. Don't think too much. See what you notice.

Exercise

Draw one of those maps. Let your imagination rule, be specific, and make a legend, something that explains what's what. (Sometimes I write all over the map as I make it.)

Exercise

Take a moment to write about what you see in this map. What did you discover in the process of drawing it?

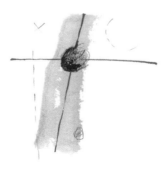

One day in the summer of 1999, two people drove up from Santa Fe to do some journal work with me in Taos. Both were feeling stuck in their creative lives, so we drew maps of those lives. The first thing one of them noticed was that his life had been full of creativity until he turned 16 and decided not to go to art school. What I noticed about my own map, was that the creative spark had remained alive in me through many years of gray darkness. While living in Europe, I was looking for the Muse in all the wrong places—and I had to laugh. My map showed me at 18 standing atop a flagpole, ready to dive into a barrel of water. In the drawing, I missed the water, missed the barrel and landed, splat, on the ground. What I realized is that my first great leap into creativity was a pratfall, not a tragedy.

I came up with this next exercise on the wing, for a conference called "Voices in the North Country," in Presque Isle, Maine. I don't live in the North Country, and I don't write about nature, yet the organizers had heard about me, and invited me to teach a one-and-a-half-hour journal workshop. I'd written a general description for the catalogue about getting in touch with our wild parts, and I had a rough idea of the kind of guided meditation I wanted to do, but I had no idea about many of the specifics. I had no idea how, or if, it would work.

I drove the eight hours north from Portland— very nearly the length of the state—in a thick fog; slowly, hunched over the steering wheel, peering through the windshield. Somewhere north of Bangor, where the highway narrows to two lanes with a suicide passing lane in the middle, I noticed that the car in front of me had a license plate that read: Odin.

Seriously.

I followed Odin through the fog, deeply grateful to this Norse God full of wisdom, poetry, and magic, who valued courage and gave us the Runes. Eventually, the fog lifted, Odin disappeared, and as I rounded a curve in the road, there was Mount Katahdin. A miracle so sudden it took my breath away. Another curve in the road, and it was gone. I couldn't find it anywhere and half thought I'd imagined it.

I got to the University of Maine at Presque Isle, parked my car, checked in at registration, grabbed a cup of coffee, and was ready to go. I introduced myself to the group and talked briefly about the benefits of keeping a journal. I wanted to get to the exercises quickly because we had so little time.

Someone raised a hand in back. "Why are we doing this?" she asked.

"Well," I said, "journals can be a useful tool to keep in touch with one's inner life…"

"I know that," said the woman. "I mean, why are we doing *this* exercise?"

The fact was, I wanted to see what would happen. I was curious if we could all go separately into the wild places in us in the same room. I was scared that it wouldn't work; we were already ten minutes into the precious time we had.

"For the hell of it," I said. "We're doing this for the hell of it. Just trust me."

Here's what we did.

Exercises

1. Draw a map of your wilderness. This could be literal, a wilderness area you already know, or it could be a metaphorical wilderness, some as yet uncharted territory of your psyche. I suggest you begin to draw without too much thought. Follow your markers, your pens, pencils, or brushes and map out the terrain; the rough spots, the smooth places, the flora and fauna. Make a legend. Name these places. Keep drawing until you feel finished.

2. Write about what you see in the map. Enter this place in your imagination. Notice the sounds, smells, and textures of things. Describe the taste in the air. Get more and more specific.

3. Notice if there are any animals in your wilderness. Take your time. Look around. Take care not to scare them off. What are these animals? Do you recognize them? Describe them and their relation to where you are in your wilderness.

4. Imagine a wild man or wild woman emerging from this wilderness. Notice the place out of which he or she steps into view. Describe this figure in as much detail as you can. Describe your interaction, your feelings, and what you sense is your relationship to this figure.

5. What message does this wilderness have for you? What communication do you get from the wild woman or wild man or the animals? Receive this message in whatever way it's given.

6. What gift is this wilderness presenting to you? Accept this gift. Describe it. Write about what it means to you.

Of course the question always comes up, "If you map wilderness is it still wilderness?" I don't know the answer. I suspect, though, that it is still wild and unknown, map or no map. Certainly the inner terrain is.

John R. Stowe, author of *The Findhorn Book of Connecting to Nature* and *Gay Spirit Warrior* sometimes talks about the plant life we find behind motels and in parking lots, growing up through cracks or in odd stretches of green around dumpsters. He urges us to look at these *between* places, closely, and there we will be surprised by how much wildness and plant spirit we discover. So, it is everywhere, this wildness; defying every attempt to map it—or even to pave it over.

Exercise

Draw a map of:

- Your past lives
- Your soul's journey
- Your spiritual path
- Your erotic life
- Your relationships
- Your body
- Your spine
- Your nervous system
- Your allergies
- Your injuries
- Your healing(s)
- Your failures
- Your challenges
- Your accomplishments
- The paths you didn't take
- Turning points in your life
- Miracles
- False starts
- Blessings
- The neighborhood you grew up in
- Your family's journey to America
- Your house
- Your future self's house
- Friendships
- Your wisdom
- Your folly

HiSTORY: MY STORY, YOUR STORY

We tell ourselves stories in order to live.

— Joan Didion

*M*aps make history. Or map makers make history. Or history changes maps. In any case, one leads to the other; they're intimately connected, maps and history. Look at the way the globe has changed since 1959—or 1989, for that matter. Cartography is a changeable business, and history, or our view of history, is far more mutable than I could've imagined in high school.

One of the great blessings of my life was the Second Wave of American Feminism, which crested as I was coming of age, and offered me, among other things, a way of looking at history and seeing my own place in it. The same was true of the Vietnam War and the Peace Movement. I discovered I had a lineage; a place in the bigger picture of thought and action, which led me to believe I also had a future.

Seeing where our personal histories connect to the histories of others and the events of our time gives us a context, a place from which to think and create and act. We have ancestors cheering us on (or hissing at us) from the heavenly wings. I think that more than anything, an awareness of history breaks down a debilitating sense of isolation. I tell my students at the art school that literature and art history are crucial because, through them, we encounter our tribe.

I'm thinking now of Rilke's *Letters to a Young Poet* or Van Gogh's letters to his brother Theo. Or a biography of Carla Moderson Becker or Kathe Kollowitz. Or Gertrude Stein's *Autobiography of Alice B. Toklas*. The painters, the poets, their diaries, letters, and biographies all remind us that someone's been here before. We have predecessors who struggled as we now struggle; who faced a blank canvas, or page, or future and didn't give up. Pick up a volume of Pablo Neruda or Sappho or Lillian Hellman, and be reminded that you're not the only one who's ever had a bad night.

So how do we get at our personal histories, and where do we begin to connect them to the bigger picture?

Begin here. At the table, a cup of coffee by my side, the morning sun streaming in the window. January thaw, 1993. Maine. I look up from my journal in time to see a flock of those small birds which seem to fly as if they were one being, dart right, then left, then shoot upward out of view.

Or begin here. It is midnight. I'm on the Channel ferry, returning to England, early December, 1977. I write in my journal about the decision I have not yet made, even though that's why I've spent the weekend in Paris with friends—to decide. And, to renew my visitor's visa in order to keep my options open. For leaving England means more than simply returning to the States; it means leaving the theater, a lover, and a life I cannot seem to fit myself into. Writing in my journal, I begin to know that, in fact, I have decided to come back to America, even as I construct another story for the customs official. Somehow I know what I've decided before knowing, though in writing, I resolve to put off the decision, resolve to wait and see. In this journal entry, I give myself a hint of the misgivings I will carry for years, and the stories I will tell myself about my life in London; stories that leave out how alone and oddly terrified I have been.

Or here. I dream about burning my notebooks. I watch page after page curl and rise through the flames. Then bits of paper with charred edges rain down from a black sky. They land on my arms and shoulders, and yet do not burn me. I pick up scraps lying on the ground and read them, trying to remember their context.

Exercise

Begin at the beginning. Tell the story of your birth. There are always stories about our birth, and they say a lot about our entry into this world. What our mothers did and did not remember, and why. Our fathers' memories. Older sisters and brothers. Grandparents. Cousins maybe. The story of your birth from all these different points of view. And what, if anything, do you remember?

Exercise

Related to your birth story is the story of how you got your name. I love beginning a workshop with this exercise because it helps me to remember who's who, and the stories themselves are great. Who were you named for? What does your name mean? Look it up if you don't know. What about nicknames? What are they, and how did you get them? How did you feel about them? How do you feel about them now? What did you do about them? Have you given yourself a name or received a new name from someone else? What's that story?

Exercise

Write about your rites of passage and turning points: Graduations, First Communion, or Bar Mitzvah. What led up to them? What were they like? How did you feel when they were over?

OH
SAY
CAN
YOU
SEE

July 4th
best favorite holiday

Exercise

Write about how you celebrated (or didn't celebrate) holidays when you were growing up. Birthdays, Chanukah, Thanksgiving, Fourth of July, Ramadan, Memorial Day, Labor Day, New Years, Yom Kippur, Easter... What is your relationship to these holidays now?

Exercise

Write about where you were and what you remember about an historical event. For example, the assassination of President Kennedy, Pearl Harbor or 9/11. Choose one and write about it. Remember as much as you can about everything you saw, heard, smelled, whom you were with, what was said, how you felt. Let the writing lead you and see what happens.

Exercise

This next exercise echoes a British documentary called *Seven Up*. Write about your best friend at age 7, and then at age 14, 21, 28, 35, 42, 49, 56, 63, 70... Or, write about your favorite clothes and the foods you loved or hated, winter boots—the list is endless. Choose a topic and write about how you felt about it at a number of different ages. Topics could include Girls, Boys, Football, Politics, and God.

Exercise

We touched upon this in the chapter on maps, and it's worth revisiting here. Draw a map of one of your old neighborhoods growing up. If you lived in the country, draw that. Who were your closest neighbors? Where was the school, the hardware store, the best climbing tree? Where was the movie theater, the taxi stand and the best hiding place? After you've drawn the map, take a minute to look at it. What do you notice? What's missing? What do size and proportion tell you? From this perspective, what is now more or less important than it was then? Write about what you see here, then keep writing as you remember more stories about your childhood; maybe when they opened the fire hydrants, or you played Capture the Flag on summer nights after supper.

Exercise

Try the same thing with the floor plan of an apartment or house you lived in as a child, and later, on your own or with roommates. Draw the map or floor plan, including details. Write about the rooms, the furniture, smells, sounds, windows, textures, drafts. Remember stories by starting with "One day," and say what happened. Go room by room. Decide on your own pattern, and see what you learn.

Exercise

Again, drawing a map if you choose, write about
various aspects of your life. The history of your life
as a cook or an athlete. Recount your life as an artist
or as an activist. Write the history of your life as a
lesbian or a father. Write the history of your body.

"We tell ourselves stories in order to live," writes
Joan Didion. This first line of her long essay called
"The White Album" has been ringing in my ears
for weeks as I have considered what it is I've been
doing in different kinds of notebooks, with varying
regularity, for the past 32 years, a practice which has
saved my life, though I'm not sure I could explain how.
The question is: can we, in the process of keeping a
journal, begin to change the stories we tell ourselves
and the stories we live?

HONORINg Our TEACHErs

Each day I long so much to see
The true teacher. And each time
At dusk when I open the cabin
Door and empty the teapot,
I think I know where he is:
West of us, in the forest.

— Francisco Albánez

translated by
Robert Bly

*I*n 1978, I returned to the States from England and started graduate studies. I'd been given a teaching fellowship. I was supposed to teach Freshman English; Composition, they called it. The University wanted me to come to a three-day seminar on the teaching of writing. I didn't have a good attitude; I was more interested in finding a place to live, and everyone was talking about this guy, Donald Murray. When I walked into his workshop, there he was: a big man with a white beard and a deep, booming voice. He talked about the writing process, and all I cared about was lunch.

Murray had us write about a person, place or thing we knew well. We were to make a list of 25 specific details and then write a few paragraphs—or maybe it was just one. Then he asked us to look back over the list and revise the paragraph. He sent us back to our rooms that evening to write something. My paragraph was about a painting teacher I'd had in high school. That evening I remembered a lot about how she stood in front of paintings; the way she talked and ate and wore her hair. I remembered the shawls she wore and how she'd sweep into the art room. She was a small woman with a huge presence; mysterious and powerful. I wrote about the years I painted with her and what I learned.

Something happened in writing that piece that changed my life forever. And I had no idea how, or what it meant. All I knew is that I'd had a writing experience that would pull me forward and inform my teaching for as long as I taught, or did anything else, for that matter. By writing, I had discovered what I didn't know I knew. I'd entered the mystery of my own mind, surrendered myself to a process, stayed with it, and completed it.

Not long after my father's death, I wrote to his best friend, thanking him for the interest he'd taken in me when I was a child. I thanked my father's friend for seeing who I was and acknowledging my interests. I thanked him for his enthusiasm and what it had taught me about being a man. My father's friend wrote back to thank me and to tell me that he'd known my father for 70 years; all his life. They'd grown up together as best friends. Still, he said he hadn't always agreed with the way my father did things. He called my father a "harsh teacher," and this opened the door for me.

It was important for me to have an outsider's view of my relationship with my father, the view of one of his contemporaries; a man who had made different choices in raising his children. Also important was that I came to value my father's harsh teachings, for one of the greatest gifts I got from my father's life was this lesson: Here is what it looks like to deny the life that is in you. Or, as the Gnostic Gospels put it, "If you do not bring forth what is within you, what is within you will destroy you." He did not one morning wake up and decide he was going to teach me this. His life taught me. For years, I charted my life in opposition to his and tried to steer clear of anything that resembled him. If my father looked disappointed or irritated about something I proposed to do, I knew I was on the right track.

Though my father's most powerful example was often a negative one, in many ways his teachings saved my life, or certainly helped me to arrive at the life I now have; a life full of challenge and contradiction, a life full of big feeling and a wide range of expression.

Exercise

List your teachers: school teachers, yes, but also authors, composers, scientists, dancers, painters, philosophers, characters in novels. Teachers you've known, and teachers you've never met in person. Feel free to include children, lovers, friends, and family members.

Now read the names of some of these teachers out loud to invoke their presence. I find this to be a powerful practice in workshops, especially speaking the names of those closest to us; those unknown to the others.

Here are some of my important teachers:

Don Murray

Dianne Benedict

Joanna Collins

Evelyn Damon

Clara Fieselman

Myra Black

Miss Hardcastle

Mitchell Johnson

Ophelia Fletcher

Odessa

Ruby

Kris Kleindienst

Sheila O'Connell

Pamela Wood

Anne Rubcam Whitten

April Werner

Paulette Valliere

William McMeniman

Self-Pity Richard

Mother

My brother

Ricki Schechter

Jonathan Aldrich

Thomas Merton

Rosa Luxemburg

Rosalie Deer Heart

Murshid Sam Lewis

Jack Mangold

Anaïs Nin

Henry Miller

Mark Twain

F. Scott Fitzgerald

Mahatma Gandhi

Dr. Martin Luther King Jr.

Malcolm X

Joan Baez

Plato

Sappho

Anne Sexton

Sylvia Plath

Adrienne Rich

Rainer Maria Rilke

Anna Akhmatova

Robert Bly

James Hillman

Flannery O'Connor

Aziza Scott

Rev. Eder

Fritz Bell

My sisters

Karl Marx

Al Gardiner

Mary Alice Hayden

Sarah Morgan

Annie Degan

Ronette Stodard

Exercise

Pick a name from your list and start writing all the stories you can think of about this teacher, everything you remember, including rumors; positive or negative and other people's stories. For example, the algebra teacher your older brother warned you about. What are your stories about teachers you loathed and came to value? How have you overcome negative influence? What did you do to rebel? How did you come to see the value in your experience? How did you rise to the great teaching of wise and compassionate people?

Exercise

Choose one of your teachers and write about the particular qualities he or she embodied, such as kindness, discipline, or enthusiasm. Tell how these qualities touched your life.

Exercise

Write a letter to one of these teachers. Say what you need to say about this teacher's impact upon you. This may be an unsent letter (or a series), or one you choose to send.

Exercise

Choose one of the teachers on your list and write a dialogue with him or her. See if you can get a fresh perspective on some question you have or a challenge you're facing.

MAnDALAS

Take your place on The Great Mandala
as it moves through your
brief moment of time.

— Peter Yarrow

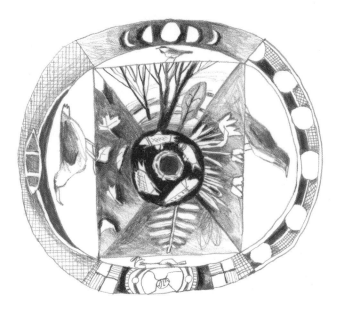

*T*here are some pretty lively debates about what a mandala is and isn't and the form it can and cannot take. Robert A. Johnson points out the importance of symmetry and sees a mandala in the way C.G. Jung saw it; as a picture of a person's soul at any given moment. Others have looser definitions and interpretations. Some people get uncomfortable with any talk of the soul, so they hold a different notion of what a mandala is. Webster's dictionary defines a mandala as a "Hindu or Buddhist graphic symbol of the universe; specif: a circle enclosing a square with a deity on each side. 2: a graphic and often symbolic pattern usu. in the form of a circle divided into four separate sections or bearing a multiple projection of an image."

One thing is clear; people have been using mandalas for centuries as a meditation tool to calm the mind and center concentration. And, for this reason, and many others, drawing them in your journal can be useful. I begin this exercise by asking people to draw a circle and then fill it in. To be asked to color within the lines is, to some, a form of oppression, so they make a point of drawing all over the page. Somehow, no matter how strong my own intent is to make symmetry, I end up wobbling here and there, but what I have in the end is an image that's always loaded with information. If I look deeply into the mandala, I can see the balances and imbalances, the so-called illness and its cure.

In one workshop I taught in St. Louis, I held up two mandalas I'd drawn as examples. The first one was dark and furious and lopsided. The second was brighter and felt more peaceful.

"Well," said one woman, "you seem to have gotten over whatever was bothering you in the first one."

It's not so much getting over something as it is externalizing an image we can use for reflection and meditation. What I often do after sitting with a mandala I've drawn is to write about what I see; the literal shapes and colors, what they suggest to me about my state of mind and my life at the moment. Sometimes these mandalas have more to say to me than others. I also like to draw them around the time of my birthday, important anniversaries, or at the solstices and equinoxes.

The most extraordinary experience I've ever had with a mandala was watching a Tibetan monk, Lobsang Samtem, make one patiently out of sand at the art school here, in Portland, Maine. The process was open to the public, and we would gather around to watch, spellbound, as he gently tapped the edge of the instruments he used to funnel colored sand into large and intricate squares, vines, rosebuds, and circles. The mandala was large, maybe five feet across, and the monk was in such a deep meditative state as he worked, more often than not the room was completely silent. Sometimes Lobsang Samtem would answer questions or talk to groups of visiting school children. And he was always cheerful.

I went to visit the day he was to sweep all the sand back together, dissolving the beautiful, rich design he'd spent so long making, and offer it as a blessing to the sea. I stood with the others while Lobsang messed up all the careful designs, poured some of the colored sand into plastic bags for personal blessings, and poured the rest into a container he would carry with us down to the docks to scatter into Casco Bay.

I felt a small anguish in my chest as I watched him disassemble his work. As a Westerner, I like to hold onto what I make, especially if I like it and think it matters, and feel it is somehow permanent. I know, it's all illusion. At the same time, I felt a remarkable sense of relief and freedom as Lobsong Samtem unmade what he'd spent so long creating. It was not an act of destruction; it was an acknowledgement of abundance and the many forms that color, light, and energy can take, the process of making and unmaking; fruition, death, rebirth.

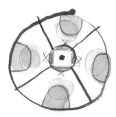

Exercise

Draw a circle. Then close your eyes for a moment. Empty your mind and breathe. When you're ready, open your eyes and start drawing with markers or crayons. Fill the space in whatever way the spirit, the hand, and the eye move you. You might draw a square inside the circle with a deity on each side, or simply follow your instincts with whatever design, images, and patterns emerge.

When you finish drawing, sit back and notice what you notice. If you feel so moved, write about what you see and discover in the mandala, or use the mandala in your meditation practice. Spend time looking at it and see what you learn.

When you draw two overlapping circles, the almond-shaped space they share is called a mandorla. In a taped lecture called *Integration and the Shadow*, Robert Johnson talks about its roots in Christian mystical practice—the Christian version of a Hindu or Buddhist mandala, if you will. One can think of this shape as the union of heaven and earth or as the space common to any two separate entities.

Last fall I taught a journal workshop called *Finding Your Life Partner*. I got the idea of distributing sheets with overlapping circles printed on them. I asked us all to fill in the shared space. I had a hunch that it would tell us something about how each of us saw partnership. I didn't limit us to the mandorla. I suggested we fill the page in whatever way felt right, but to pay particular attention to that almond shape in the center.

It was fascinating to see what we all did with it. Some started drawing from the outside, in; outside the circles, from the edges of the page. Others focused on the mandorla, ignoring everything else. Some managed to show how each circle was unique and what each contributed to the shape they shared, so that the mandorla was not only made up of the material of each circle, but was also a thing unto itself; connected and related, but distinct.

After we'd finished drawing, I asked, "What does this tell you about how you view relationships?" By focusing on the images before us, we could articulate our beliefs about partnership in a whole new way. I invite you to do the same.

Exercise

Draw two circles that overlap. Then fill in the spaces in any way that interests you. When you've finished, sit back and reflect on what you see. What do these circles, especially where they overlap in the mandorla, tell you about your perception of partnership? How does this compare to your experience? Take some time to write about what you notice.

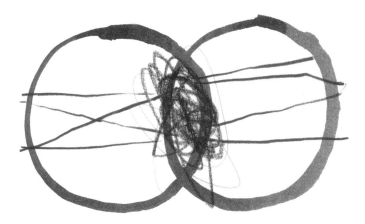

Kinship, Community: What We Have in Common

Cedar waxwings will pass blueberries one to
another, until each has fed.

— from *North Country
Weather & Wildlife
Calendar, 1984*

I often forget how much courage it takes to show up for a journal workshop. When I first started going to classes and workshops myself, I was petrified. So I'm careful to acknowledge the bravery of those who arrive on the first night and am conscious of creating a safe place for us all. A regular journal workshop is one thing, but one in which we are looking at what we want in a life partner is quite another, in terms of the level of risk and vulnerability. The experience of this recent workshop was an astonishing one, and with the permission of the participants, I wanted to talk about it here for the light it sheds on community.

That there were any men in the group at all was unusual, but that these particular guys showed up was a blessing. If I remember correctly, two of them had engineering backgrounds and the other was a landscaper. The women were every bit as remarkable: a mathematician, a bookseller, an artist, and a divinity student. All of them, men and women, were adventurers.

The first night was fine. Born under the sign of Aries, I always love the beginning of anything. We started with the overlapping circle exercise. I'd brought in blank books for everyone and invited them to make the books their own. Both the bookseller and the artist were accomplished and enthusiastic makers of collage, so they were off and running. The mathematician looked worried. I began in the usual ways by outlining the eight weeks, and drawing up some group agreements; a list of what we all needed from the group in order to do what we'd gathered to do.

The next week, our second class, I pitched us all headlong into the soup without intending to. We focused on gremlins (you remember gremlins). So we began drawing and naming our gremlins around dating. The atmosphere in the room grew thick and heavy, almost viscous. I opened a window even though it was the middle of February. We were nearing the point at which each of us finds a way to overcome the gremlin and proceeds with greater confidence and a lighter heart.

But not this night. For some reason, we could not get bigger than our gremlins. People seemed to feel they *were* their gremlins. Nothing I said seemed to help. Then the class was over; it was time to go. Everyone appeared deeply depressed. I'd botched it. Walking home that night, I told myself this class was the worst idea I'd ever had. In other words, I walked home in the company of my own teaching gremlins.

The next week we lightened up a lot, writing about what our ideal partnership would look like. Then one of the men (I'll call him Mike) tossed his pen onto the table, shook his head and said, "Look, all this talk about ideals is nice, but it's really a load of horse shit. You know what I really want? It doesn't make me proud, but what I really want is a woman who'll bring me my beer when I'm watching the basketball game on TV. Someone who'll protect my addictions."

There was a silence in the room. He'd said the unutterable, voiced the unthinkable. I think all of us understood what had happened. There'd been a movement of Grace in his speaking up right then. He'd told the truth not only on himself but to some extent on all of us, no matter what our politics or preferences. And we got it. He'd named the thing we'd all been dancing around; a desire to be in relationship so we could hide from the world and all the bigger possibilities of what we could be in that world. We acknowledged the presence of our collective shadow; owned it. There was room for it in our circle. And once it was out in the open, we could proceed with the rest of our work. We were all grateful to Mike for keeping us honest, and in doing so, opening up more space for us all.

An extraordinary thing had happened, something that happens so often in groups that I've come to expect it, and yet I'm always amazed when it shows up. Group wisdom took over and presented us with a difficult truth. We saw it in each other, and in ourselves. We were stunned, maybe even frightened, and then we laughed out loud to welcome it in. Some weeks later, in an exercise in which we were listing different perspectives from which we could view dating, it was Mike who once again gave us what we needed. I'd been writing down all the possible perspectives on a flip chart; "I'm too old." "There's nobody out there for me." "This is a waste of time." "Love is mystical; we shouldn't be messing with it." "This is a challenge." "What are the possibilities?" Then Mike's face brightened and he said, "I have one. How about, 'Even a blind pig can find an acorn once in a while.'" And so we added it to the list.

Toward the end of the course, a guy in my men's group asked, "So has anyone found a life partner yet?"

"No," I said. "But everyone knows a lot more about who they are, what's important to them, and what they're looking for in a relationship." I thought of the woman who had come to realize how many relationships she had in her life whether or not she was dating. Another woman had discovered how important solitude is to her. Another man was all set and ready to start dating again. No one had found a life partner, but everyone had found their life.

Whether it's for six hours on a Saturday, or two hours every Tuesday evening for eight weeks, what we do in a journal workshop is to form community, a powerful one with deep connections. We regularly break down old notions and open up new possibilities. We're nothing to do with measuring up, or matriculating, or improving our resumes—none of that. We're up to something far more important— nothing less than cultivating wildness and keeping the inner life alive. And that's exactly what I hope this handbook is helping you to do.

People are often surprised and delighted by what happens in these groups of strangers who come together in a seeming random selection. I say *seeming* because there's a curious logic to it. I've noticed this again and again and have come to appreciate this connectedness, for I'm not a man who has had much use for community in his life—at least that's the story I've told myself.

I'm a lone wolf, always have been, and I've never wanted anything much to do with groups, feeling confined or constrained by them in what I now recognize as a classic, American male way. But as I've grown older, I realize that I've always hungered for community, connectedness with others, my kind, a pack or tribe. I never felt I really had one and felt ambivalent about them when I'd been involved in them. I have finally come to see that I have never not been in a community of one kind or another; something of a revelation for a lone wolf.

My first community was, of course, the family I was born into, the people I used to pretend weren't related to me. In my fantasy, my brother and sisters were fellow actors and circus performers, and my parents were nice people who ran the boarding house where we all happened to be living. Then of course there was school. My grade school was called Community School, and I walked to it every day and often played on the playground on weekends and summers. In those days, community had everything to do with what was local and, in my case, what was within walking distance. I am still that way about where I live. I need to be able to walk to the grocery store, to work and to the bookstores, so I arrange my life that way. It's how I define where I live and what I mean by community.

Exercise

How do you define community? Describe some of the various communities you've lived in. What made them communities to you? Where did they succeed? And where did they fail?

Exercise

If you could design the perfect community, what would it look like? How would people live? What would the houses be like? What would your relationships with your neighbors be? What form of government would you have? How would young people be educated?

I'm a traveler. I move around a lot. Between 1970 and 1982, I lived in seven different states and three foreign countries. Since 1990, I've made three trips to Russia and visited Estonia, Poland, the Czech Republic, Canada, and India. In 1995, I began a yearly summer migration to northern New Mexico to write and teach, returning to Maine in the fall. My primary community is in Maine, where I've lived for 22 years, but I have other communities as well. I've come to see myself as what you might call inter-tribal; which is to say, I pass between, visit, carry messages and link one group to another, without staying on to become a member of either.

Wherever I go, I end up participating in the lives of the people in some way, or I feel lost and without purpose. Work of some kind—more often than not a journal workshop—connects me to a place. I gather people together, and we dive into our inner lives. Or I sit in ceremony with them and join them in prayer. When I taught for a month in Estonia, I went most mornings to the Russian Orthodox church to pray before class. Many evenings, I went to the theater— often because I was alone and afraid; the political situation was deeply unsettled that spring. Never mind that I understood not a word of what was said on stage, I was there doing what we have done for tens of thousands of years; gathering together to watch a public dream, to witness a part of our collective story unfold.

In the past 12 years or so, the men's movement has become important to me. Circles of men, circles of gay men especially, have been a real lifeline, and the communities they have engendered continue to grow and change and support men all over the world. I don't remember exactly when I started leading journal workshops for men, but I do remember the sense of coming home I felt in that first circle, where we wrote about our fathers. What do men talk about when we gather? Not just women, and not just getting laid, no matter what our sexual preference. No. We talk about our relationship to other men, our fathers, sons, brothers, grandfathers, friends, teammates, lovers, and rivals. We talk about competition and work and money and sex and love and spirit and animals and sport and our bodies and injuries and victories and death. And that's what we write about in men's journal workshops.

Though my men's group in Maine is not a journal group, we write together. We gather for pot luck supper every other Wednesday. After we eat, we clear the table and engage in a practice called Proprioceptive Writing, which was taught to us by Tobin Simon and Linda Trichter Metcalf (See Resources for Journal Keepers after this chapter). The point is, we make this time for ourselves, book it way in advance, and mostly we show up. We take our time together seriously. Wives, work, children, girlfriends, boyfriends, are set aside for those evenings, and we practice being in community, getting still, listening to our own minds, and letting each other in on our thoughts.

What we have in common is the diving in. We are also men of a certain age, facing questions about fatherhood, childlessness, the changes in our bodies, being in love, partnership, loss, being available to aging parents or friends who are dying, and the question of how to become a conscious elder.

Finally, and ironically, what I've learned by leading workshops is that keeping a journal is no longer enough for me. The practice has provided me with a space, a temple, a rehearsal hall, and I've come to see its value more and more in how I am able to move out of the notebooks with the insights they contain, and step back into the world, meeting its wildness with my own.

Our task, then, is to build strong containers for our inner lives, so we can be even more spirited participants in the world and its changes. True, most of us need more time alone. It's also true that many of us long for new ways of being with each other. So we form drumming groups, New Moon Circles, prayer groups, dance circles, 12-step fellowships, book groups, writers groups, journal groups. I say let's keep forming them, modifying them, dissolving them when they no longer serve us, and inventing them all over again. Let's continue to commit whole-heartedly to this experiment and see if we can, indeed, continue to husband the wildness in ourselves and in the world.

Resources for Journal Keepers

Adams, Kathleen. *Mightier Than the Sword: The Journal as a Path to Men's Self-Discovery*. Warner Books.

Baldwin, Christina. *Life's Companion*. Bantam Books.

Cameron, Julia. *The Artist's Way*. Tarcher/Putnam.

Carson, Richard. *Taming Your Gremlin*. HarperCollins.

Deer Heart, Rosalie. *Harvesting Your Journals*. Heart Link Publications, Inc.

Goldberg, Natalie. *Writing Down the Bones* and *Wild Mind*. Bantam Books.

Johnson, Alexandra. *The Hidden Writer: Diaries and the Creative Life*. Anchor Books.

Mallon, Thomas. *A Book of One's Own: People and their Diaries*. Hungry Mind Press.

Alexandra Merrill (Percept Language), 19 Glad Farm Road, St. George, Maine 04860.

Metcalf, Linda and Tobin Simon. *Writing the Mind Alive: The Proprioceptive Method for Finding Your Authentic Voice.* Bantam Books.

Progoff, Ira. *At A Journal Workshop: Writing to Access the Power of the Unconscious and Evoke Creative Ability.* Tarcher/Putnam.

Thompson, Jason. *Making Journals by Hand: 26 Creative Projects for Keeping Your Thoughts.* Quarry Books.

Vaughan, Joy. *Off the Edges & Outside the Lines: a Guide to Making Meaningful Personal Images.* Available by writing to P.O. Box 200, South Bristol, Maine 04568.

Walker, Leslie Clare. *Keeping a Nature Journal: Observing, Recording, Drawing the World Around You.* Storey Books.